Raw and Personal without Apology

Raw and Personal without Apology

Daryl Ross Halencak

8TH STREET PRESS
BOOKS BY PEGGY BROWNING & FRIENDS
8thstreetpress.com

Copyright 2022 Daryl Ross Halencak
All rights Reserved
ISBN: 9798840899472
Book Design by Peggy Browning
Published by 8th Street Press

Foreword

The poems offered between these covers are, as the title of the book suggests, raw. Not raw in the sense of underprepared or unfinished, nor—as members of my and the author's generation may think, recalling the widely-successful comedy album of a young Eddie Murphy—unrelentingly vulgar and profane (not that either are bad things in general and certainly not in poetry), but raw in the sense of brutally-honest.

As Halencak makes clear in his poetic introduction—an introduction that is just as much invocation as anything else— "In this collection, I exposed/ myself and the world I live in." An exposure that is unrelenting, unflinching, with two clear goals in mind.

The first goal is to allow Halencak—to borrow a phrase from Walt Whitman—to sound his barbaric yawp over the rooftops of the world. Again, from the introductory poem, Halencak stands before us "exposed," "naked," offering his full and total self for our scrutiny. And it is a self well worth scrutinizing.

I first met Daryl during a reading of the Woody Guthrie Poets in Oklahoma City in 2017. He was a strident voice offering a defense of the menial, the underrepresented; a voice full of anger and defiance, taking the suffering and anger of those underrepresented and downtrodden and making it his (not a total surprise from a former lawyer, I suppose).

I would meet him a second time the next year, also in Oklahoma City, where I was progressing through the Red Earth M.F.A. program. Daryl was taking advantage of the program's day pass, giving him access to workshops and to the comradery, the program is so well known for. At that point, I knew him only as the firebrand from the Woody Guthrie readings. That day, those of us in the workshops were treated to additional layers within Daryl: deep, abounding humanity, a clear, infectious zest for life, and a reflexive empathy to those around him. As these poems make clear, he knows suffering, intimately, and so has committed himself to nip the suffering of others in the bud when and as soon as he can. On that day, we became fast friends, fully supporting each other's work we can.

I mentioned above that Daryl's intentional, raw self-exposure seems to have two goals in mind. The second of these is a deep desire to make the reader uncomfortable. He is unwilling to accept the world—and its casual tolerance for suffering—as it is. He demands a better one. And he demands that we demand it as well. While Daryl is adept at words—as these poems will clearly show—his true medium is discomfort. He is a master, a maestro at making us uncomfortable, for it is only through discomfort—collective and individual—that change becomes a real possibility.

This brings us to the back half of the title of this book. This collection is not just raw, it is unapologetic. Daryl asks no permission he curries no favor, and begs no forgiveness, for there is nothing to forgive. Like the long brother- and sisterhood of protest poets before him, he does not ask, he demands. He will wear our discomfort like a favorite hat, treating our shuffling feet, our awkward glances skyward, our mildly-embarrassed throat clearings, as his just due, as the proper payment for the poet of our collection conscience (But this is not Abbie Hoffman, so buy the book—although a part of me thinks Daryl would be just fine with you stealing it if the theft came with a promise to read and deeply-think upon it).

I would end by expressing a hope that you will find these poems as disturbing, challenging, and profoundly beautiful as I did, but that is, to a very real extent, like hoping you'll find the sun warm and the rain wet. Instead, I will merely congratulate you and send a "fare thee well" your way.

--Professor Paul Juhasz, Seminole Oklahoma State College

Poetic Introduction of Raw and Personal without Apology

I felt my soul,
synthesized beauty and felt at peace —
all this by reading your book.

Earth opened to show
a western star on your horizon
seeping farther into a temblor,
further into thought.

A storm came and was swallowed
by cracks spewing tiny islands
from granules of sand fallen,
spurred by coyotes running across prairie.

I heard the silence of days
rumble where buffalo thunder on the ground.
Words of lightning splintered the sky.

Seedlings fell into rifts
of shifted earth.
The rain lifted them to the surface
where desert flowers grow.

--James Coburn, spring of 2022

*James Coburn is a noted journalist, international writer, poet,
and activist for important social and political issues.

Preface

In this collection of poetry, I exposed
myself and the world I live in
      the past,
        the future,
      the present.

I have no apologies.
No regrets.
I'm raw and naked.

Dedication

Jane, I thank you for everything you've given to me.

You're an advocate, activist, caregiver,
and my best friend.

You have my back.

Acknowledgments

I gratefully acknowledge those who helped with my artistic soul and poetry:

The late poet, activist, publisher, and writer Judge Dorothy Alexander who keeps me sane with her love and mentorship; artist and activist Devy Napier; poet Professor Jessica Isaac; poet, musician, Oklahoma Poet Laureate Professor Nathan Brown; Canadian poet and photographer Andrew Scott; poet and writer Professor Dr. Julie Chappell; Professor Hank Jones; poet and writer Professor Dr. Ken Hada; poet and journalist James Coburn; poet and writer Professor Ron Wallace; poet and writer Professor Dr. Timothy Bradford; poet, writer, and poet Professor Paul Juhasz; poet Linda Smith; poet Sheri Sutton, and those assisted in my artistic life.

D.A. Kitchens photographer: cover art

Photographer and local historian: Jim Rich
The Center a/Town, Rolling On, Mighty Pease River

Musician and photographer: Kelsey Lien
The Tuba Beat

Photographer: Jim Livingston Art
Saint Joseph's Catholic Church

Book Design: Peggy Browning, 8th Street Press

Books by Daryl Ross Halencak

Staring Blue Eyes
Land on the Other Side
Rolling Across the Plains
poetry. passion. life.

All books are available on amazon.com

Don't use the telephone.
People are never ready to answer it.
Use poetry.

--Jack Kerouac, 1970

Contents

Foreword 5
Poetic Introduction of Raw and Personal without Apology 7
Preface 9
Dedication 11
Acknowledgments 12
Books by Daryl Ross Halencak 13
My Lover, My Friend 19
last kiss in our sacred space 20
Angry Voice 21
I Speak my Mind 22
Blasphemy! 23
The Abandoned Child 24
Brothers Across Pease River 25
The Stranger 26
Bar with an Attitude 27
Funeral 28
Pickled Eggs 29
Distant Mounds 30
Waiting for Children to Come Home 31
Turd Farm 32
How Do You Spell It? 33
Life and Times of Crippled Scar Face 34
The Outdoor Toilet 35
1619 Jamestown 36
Tornado Alley 37
Actress in the Red Dress 38
Mountain Oysters 39
Trail Beyond Ground Zero 40
Blowing Pioneers 41
Shutters Allow the Sun 42
My Ross Family's Margaret Methodist Church 43
Under the Moonlight 44
The Killer 45

Banquet 1934	46
Chop Weeds, Clean the Pool on Main Street	47
From a Shoebox in the Attic	48
We Are Sharecroppers	49
Septic Tears	50
Flatlands Poet	51
Poem for Music Man	52
What Would Ginsberg Do	53
Pennies in a Jar	54
Campsite Stories	55
Damn the Darkness	56
Looking for the Light	57
Faces	58
Hoover Texas	59
This Place	60
Contemplation in Summer	61
Man, I've Got the Beat	62
Visions on Medicine Mounds	63
Pleasures	64
Fiery Hell	65
My Mesquite Tree	66
Thunder Clouds	67
Dark Night Sky	68
Margaret's Sandy Loam	69
Where Planted	70
Not Give In	71
Picture	72
Addiction Is My Name ***	73
Harvest	74
I Thirst	75
Opened	76
Black Hole	77
Poet's introduction to his haiku	78
The Center of Town	83

Roll On, Mighty Pease	84
The Tuba Beat	86
Dying Gaul	87
Saint Joseph's Catholic Church	88
Grand Finality	90
Fragility	91
My Czechoslovak Grandparents	92
Time Moving On	93
White Side of Town	94
Ants Before the Storm	95
sine die	96
Book Club Discussion Questions	98
About the Poet	99

My Lover, My Friend

I hope you find this letter under
our favorite tree.
Where are you?
I listen for sounds of laughter.
I look for you in the nighttime
shine. No luck.
Did you visit the riverbanks? Are
you the rainbow clouds?
Are you over the rainbow, through the shadows?
See beyond the covered sun tonight?
I search for you under the glimmer of the western sky.
Will you see the silver eye of the smiling dusk?
Can you taste the cherry wind?
Smell the flowers of the dream
river?
Touch the azure field, tucked under the gentle
dew? We would wonder if life is fleeting;
hear the silent brook rolling into
eternity. Will you and I chase the
somber meaning and be on the same
path?

Yes, we shall, when we find each other, again.

last kiss in our sacred space

travels will not separate
love, tenderness, mystical
embraces, or fond memories
in our sacred space even
though we have different
endings

forever together tastes
    powerful, explosive kisses within
us but if not,
we'll remember how we
loved
    one last time
        in our sacred space

eternity
will record our love
    no beginning
    no end

one last kiss
        in our sacred space
before the cattle car
    doors

        close

Angry Voice

I found my father in a deserted park,
remembering his childhood.
Once,
he was full of vigor and mirth.
His muscled arms were
strong. He soared over the
mountains.

It was cold.
He was a butterfly at the first
freeze. My father was alone,
entering the last winter.
When his eyes were open,
he gazed at a pile of
leaves-
       brittle
        discarded.
Life was ending.

Nature rehearsed the dirge.
A choir of naked branches sang in
unison. It was the final opera.
He knew it.
       Falling leaves-
           angry
           feeble
           dying.

The ones who have a voice must speak
for those who are voiceless.
-*Archbishop Oscar Romero*

I Speak my Mind

The radical removes his bandages each morning
and enters the arena to begin another battle.
Bruises are his prize.
He shouts:

I speak my mind.

Free speech continues the war
through the valley of the unblemished and untarnished.
This bloody warrior is unabashed.
He raises fists and screams:

I speak my mind!

Though tortured and whipped,
 he keeps walking,
crawling,
crying:

I speak my mind!

He does not find holiness,
only madness.
His vision remains intact
and proclaims:

I speak my mind!

       He is Oscar Romero.
       He is Martin Luther King.
       He is Everyman and
        Everywoman with a voice.

Blasphemy!

Do you know who I
am?
My name is Revolution.
Blasphemer.
Activist.
Poet.
I fight for older people and the
disabled; children waiting for the
next meal;
    people of color.
Poets march into
Hell
-with conviction
-with words and actions.
The social order tries to silence agitators,
 like me.
I speak my mind regardless of the
consequences. I am a radical poet.
Blasphemy!

The Abandoned Child

I am a child, seeking a
home, a refugee,
facing the lake of fire.
My parents were killed because
they were born on the wrong
side of eternity.
Our family was told to
believe in the land of milk
and honey and to pray for a
new Paradise.

Nothing.

I am running toward the
mirage, but it is a sea of hot
sand, needing a sip of water.
I walk west or north but
the golden key turned to rust.

There is no place to
 go.
No place to hide.

I am a child
refugee.
My parents are
dead.

But Jesus said, Suffer little children, and forbid them not, to come unto me: for of such is the kingdom of heaven.
Matt. 19:4 KJV

Brothers Across Pease River

Devin and Andrew sat in silence on the homestead porch watching the
full moon over the river.
There was stillness, except for the wind blowing across the Rolling
Plains. Andrew broke the unsettling tenor of the evening,
"First full moon of the summer."
Devin looked straight ahead and pretended that he did not hear his
younger brother's words.
Growing up, Devin was the one needing nothing except everything.
Spoiled.
Sulking when he did not get his way.
Always acting like a child.
Andrew was adopted, and, from the first day the infant
arrived, Devin refused to accept him.
There were never two brothers as opposite.
Andrew gave in, often, to his brother's demands to save family peace.
Now, after their parent's funeral, they were forced to be together, watching
the full moon rising.
Fascination with the skies was the only thing the brothers had in
common growing up;
and now, they were together with the object both had loved
for a lifetime.
Devin broke his silence: "What about Dad's coin collection?"
Caught off guard, Andrew slowly turned to face his brother and told him that their father
had given him the collection several years ago.
Devin kept staring at the moon with his usual stone-cold glare.
"You are going to at least split them with me, right?"
Andrew quietly, yet defiantly, replied "no."
Andrew slowly turned his face back to the moon, now becoming a
brilliant red glow in the dark sky.
The loneliness of the duo was like the dark palls placed over the
caskets just a few hours prior.
Andrew's grief seemed to lift a bit within brotherly silence and coldness.
"full moon means it will rain."
Silence. *

"I am not I; thou art, not he or she; they are not they."
Evelyn Waugh, BRIDESHEAD REVISITED, 1944

The Stranger

I gazed at the stranger's
tombstone in the Old Margaret Cemetery.
He had died in the 1880s
when the old town
full of residents,
outlaws, and travelers
going to greener
pastures.

Now, his life whispers
within the burial ground.
The stranger is not remembered,
except for the tombstone.

I have visions of his body
blowing his life into the sandy land.
Perhaps he had a wife?
What kind of horse did he ride?
Did he have black hair and hazel
eyes? Was he tall and lean?
Was he a saloonkeeper in Old Margaret?

I wonder whether he was a
cowboy or a farmer sweating in
the dryland cotton fields.

His days were done.
His visions have ceased
and his soul saddled up and rode
into the sunset.

Bar with an Attitude

I sat down at a broken table in a Communist
bar in the mountains of the Czech Republic.
I wandered off from the other tourists for
a pint of warm, flat pivo
and a cup of Turkish coffee, full of grounds.
I found the nearest pivovar and it was dingy and
dirty, but I had a powerful thirst.
The tavern was full of workers after the workday.
Over the tables, I saw pictures of Lenin, Stalin, and a tattered naked
woman. Men and boys were full of conversation until I entered the
pivovar.

                              Silence.

In my rusty Czech language, I ordered a pint of Budvar, my favorite
beverage. I smile with the beer in my hand, stammered a salutation,
dobra rano.
I spoke the phrase incorrectly, but the Communists understood what I
tried to say. I raised the glass and lift it toward the other table.
They responded and they were confused.
I finished my pivo and I ordered a cup of Turkish coffee-- strong,
black, full of coffee grounds.
Now, Communists looked at me and I smiled.
They responded.

I was not in danger because they knew I tried to act
like a wandering Bohemian, looking for my
background,
love pivo,
and strong Turkish coffee.

Funeral

Locals called him Bug,
    indigent,
        white trash,
            dirty.

County Judge decided to
 bury Bug in the indigent
plot-blowing sand, full of
weeds.
After Bug's death,
his son bought new black clothes--
the first time he had worn a suit.
The funeral director did his best:
shaved and prepped for the viewers.
Before the service,
The drunks passed the hat.
Bug would have liked it.
When the preacher man saw them
huddled together,
He glared at this
    gathering: He
    hated drunkards.
        He hated dirty,
            white trash.
The unholy man delivered his usual sermon for
sinners:
        Burning coals are for sinners.
        Hallelujah!
        Jesus is coming!
        The Lord says
        "REPENT!"

He screeched loud, Bible-inspired words, with a Texas twang.
    No one was listening.
The crowd waited for the end of his story of Hell.
    Bug was dead.
No one cared-
        except
            white trash.

Pickled Eggs

Work's over and I'm
tired and horny.
Time for cold beer-
salty peanuts
my cutie
and a few pickled eggs.
I've got quarters for the jukebox to
slide on the floor with my gal-
cheek-to-cheek
eyes closed
smelling her sweet cologne.
Yep, I'11 get happy this Friday night.
Paychecks are handed at 5:00 so
I'll drive my old pick-up, pass Main Street,
and stop at my gal's house.
She'll wonder how my pick-up scraped
on the left fender.
I'll tell her the tree got in the way.
She'll buy it.
When I'll pick her up
I want to kiss her in front of the
neighbors. I'll not be embarrassed.
Not at all.
They'll know we're headed to the dancehall
and beer joint across the Red River to Trash
Hill Oklahoma. I'll find rot-gut 3.2 green
beer -
tasty for this ole field hand.
You know, it's not a sin for me, but my gal's preacher told her
drinking beer is the best way to Hell Fires.
Oh well, we'll find out.
Workweeks are long and the weekends are too
short. But tonight, I'll waltz the floor with my gal
cheek-to-cheek
smelling her sweet cologne
eyes closed
condoms in my pocket.

Maybe I'll be lucky.

Distant Mounds

Over the rolling plains, the regiment
found Medicine Mounds.
Emaciated folk starving
wild plums and edible
plants to sustain hungry
bellies-easy targets for
rifles.

Sul Ross' soldiers looked for
Chief Quanah Parker but he was
not found. -he traveled far from
Pease River in search of bison.

Soldiers saw the camp and tasted blood.
Thundering horses murdered
the vulnerable and the stench of death
Was the dark pall under the western sky.
Swords of genocide cleansed
the small band of women and children
huddled at the edge of the
flowing, bloody Pease River.

Waiting for Children to Come Home

My neighbor lady plants plastic flowers.
Her garden was once lovely but
now, it's full of Dime Store geraniums.
She lives in the home she raised her children
and believes it is safe, but it is not.
The neighborhood is different.
Dinners are delivered from her church, checking on her if she had
fallen.
Before bedtime, she watches television
without conversation.
Her restless slumbers
are punctuated by her cries.
Her children were chasing the American Dream
and they left her alone.
No one will plant germaniums in her yard
and she is waiting for her children to come
home.

Turd Farm

Turd Farm was a unique hang-out
for old men playing dominoes.
No idea why it was named Turd
Farm. It was a haven in the 1960s
and 1970s.
With nothing to do,
they congregated in the tin building
next to the sewer treatment plant.
That's right -next to the sewer treatment plant.
It must have not bothered them.
Played games.
drank beer.
sometimes, guggled whiskey.
Cussed.
Spat.
Told tall tales.

Now, they are all dead,
flying in the clouds with harps
and crooked haloes around Turd
Farm in the sky.

How Do You Spell It?

How do you spell it
when life is upside
down,
and symptoms follow it along the way,
pain, and confusion?
It spells loneliness within my mind, within my body,
without freedom, and faculties.

How:
-can I spell it when words don't make sense?
-when I can't stand?
-when I can't grasp a fork?
-or control bodily functions?
-when I lose my way?

I am not the village idiot,
living within Beckett's play,
Waiting for Godot*?

The disease doesn't define me-
    not my speech
       not hobbling
          not falling
             not confusion.

      I'm on my path and it is just fine.

One of the central themes of the play and book, "Waiting for Godot" is the human condition. As homeless tramps, Vladimir and Estragon represent those who have been left behind by society: the elderly, the poor, and the infirm, who feel as though they've been abandoned by God and doomed to lives of misery and discontent.

Life and Times of Crippled Scar Face

The guy named Scar Face did not hang out
with the Homecoming Queen.
His old Chevy was too decent for a whore, especially this one.
Since the wreck, she laughed at his scars and
limp. She often said" damn, cripple, you are ugly
as sin" and walks away.
She hurts his soul.
He hates her guts,
but he could not
miss
the Grand Entrance of the Year.
The winning team and the coach lusted for
the Star of the Show.
The Queen licked her ruby lips and winked.
Her teeth were aspirin white with her pristine
China Doll Face. The packed stadium drooled
for Marilyn Monroe's Street Walker
Demeanor.
She curled eyelashes for the event,
but not for Scar Face.
Her head was crowned and placed on her curls,
then left the field, arm-in-arm with the quarterback.
Scar Face stared at the couple as
they walked to the gym for the fifth
quarter victory party.
"Guess the quarterback will be lucky tonight."
After the game,
Scar Face left with a case of beer
and drove around the back roads.
Drunk.
Smoked a joint or
two

Alone.

The Outdoor Toilet

Before we left our cotton patch home
and moved into our new house in the
Margaret community,
My first privy was in the middle of
our irrigated farm, close to "Farm-
to-Market Road 98."
It was an outdoor toilet,
constructed of second-hand
lumber with
green shingles on the roof.
I would sneak off, climb the structure
and become an action hero.
Inside, the tissue hung on a
nail low enough for a child,
high enough for an adult.
I was curious why the excrement
was covered with lime.
(I thought limes were for human
consumption). I didn't know that the
stench was putrid, nothing bad could be
associated with my Empire State Building.
On top, I became
Superman: I saved the
world.
I could fly.

1619 Jamestown

In the year of our Lord 1607, I praise willing souls who
    followed dreams of freedom, and humanity's potential.
I praise forefathers and mothers who searched for heaven-on-
    earth, ripe for equality.
I praise the pearl of great price where settlers snuggled in safe
    beds for the first time after the Puritan war.
Faith praises answered prayers for a new way of life,
    smelling fresh air, and peace.
In the year of our Lord 1619, Pilgrim
Calvinists spiraled into destruction,
stumbled into their type of
    tyranny.
Slavery shackled precious human values, and
    Christian beliefs were compromised.
In the year of our Lord four centuries
    later, I cry, I scream, I am angry:
    do "Black Lives Matter,"
    do they, "say-their-
    names",
    do homeless folk live on
    the street and do children live in
    cages?
I question:
will despair end, my dear Republic?
Holy Scriptures set forth-- *Faith without works is dead.*
In the year of our Lord in the future,
I long for change and democracy for all.
My hymn, our refrain will sing from the highest hill:

                    One Nation under God Indivisible
                       with Liberty and Justice
                              for All.

Tornado Alley

Southwestern clouds roll onto the dry
plains, ushering in hurricane-force winds.
The Heavens appear like a swirling mix of
 brown, grey, and green
as Mother Nature prepares her assault.
Death Angels focus on telescopic sights
on rural villages and suburban cul-de-sacs.
Scanning the horizon, families observe the
voodoo talismans announcing the time for
entrance into underground shelters. Those
without root cellars or concrete bunkers huddle
together in disheveled interior closets.
Most are filled with children's
clothes and Sunday go-to-meeting suits
hanging onto wooden rods.
Interior shelters prove to be flimsy protective mantillas,
covering cowering families.
Fears grasp the residents like the clutches of circling
hawks to unprotected rodents.
And then, like the ominous blast in Nagasaki, it hits.
It hits with a fury, with anger and malicious intent.
Once on the ground, the tornado sounds
like a freight train crashing into a brick wall.
Metal sheets wrap around ancient buildings
as Christmas tinsel hung from a Christmas tree.
Semi-trucks are thrown around like
baseballs at a little league game.
There is no game-- only destruction and death.
Bloody bodies tossed about within the storm's funnels.
Homes with families inside are leveled.
Mighty trees collapse onto the underground shelters.
Even those cloistered within the earth are
neither safe nor saved.
The gods of the skies have their way,
as the world watches the
drama played out on the
Weather Channel.

Actress in the Red Dress

The frozen line outside the
theater was ready.
The Russian press anticipated
her appearance
in the red dress
 and ruby lips.
The former President's
sexual expression mattered:
Trump was in love.
The audience was required to
comment on her demeanor.
She was
beautiful.
She knew it.
It was time to begin.
It was opening night with her
name in lights on the marquee.
The thespian captured the
Moscow production.
Executives cast a soulless
mannequin.
Great for the dialogue.
Trump caught her eye.
The actress performed
for the former
President. She smiled
at the former Circus
Clown
in the first row.
Trump was
mesmerized.
She blew wet kisses.
She did her part.

Mountain Oysters

I despised cutting testicles out of young
bulls to make ready for the sales barn in
Vernon, Texas, or Hollis Oklahoma.
I've done it since I was a child.
Until 1996, I raised cattle on my family's
pasture, near Pease River.
When a man like myself raised
cattle, the herd owner and the hired
hands sliced and pulled out the
testicles
of the calves.
(Steers sold better than bulls.)
Once removed, we threw nasty organs
on a thin sheet over the branding fire
and ate the balls after work.
I'm sure I drank a six-pack.
Had to.
I imagined the meal helped me
to be a better lover.
It didn't.
I was in charge and looked like a cowboy.
The virile young pup hired hands ate
that stuff like a real man.
Finger licking is good.
I thought that I was a real
man, the owner in charge,
and my position demanded to
chew and swallow the Mountain
Oysters I did it.
Now, I've told the story.
Thank God I sold my cows in 1996.
I didn't like riding horses, fixing
fences, and cutting testicles out of
poor calves anyway.

Trail Beyond Ground Zero

I didn't sleep well.
Nightmares circled my ground zero.
Dreams haunted my world.
I thought Inferno would be
darkness and depression.
I dreamt Demons dragged my life
through torture and blood.
Perhaps Hell was my predestination.
It was not.
I woke from my slumbers,
amazed at the brilliant
colors,
and found the trail beyond
compare. My soul traveled in
fields.
My bare feet felt soft earth.
Tasted the warm breeze.
Smelled fields of ripe grain.
No Pain.
No
violence.
No sickness.
Only beauty and rest, new heaven;
new earth.

Blowing Pioneers

Saddling fierce
winds Blowing
sands
Rolling down to the rivers
Sailing with blazing parched skin of sallow families,
scorching oceans of sage, and mesquite
Drought smelling the fury
as the wagons trailed toward the western sun
Crying for safe harbors with thirsting hearts

Dreaming minds for a new start,
      new visions of the new
         place for home--their
         home

Shutters Allow the Sun

I'll open shutters allowing the sun's
radiance. New day's portal opens, pour a
cup of coffee, then smile, chasing night's
shadows.
It's time for
reflective moments
in mornings alone,
       silence with my thoughts,
      pen in hand, scripting
          adventure,
          blessings,
          prayers,
             fresh experiences.

My Ross Family's Margaret Methodist Church

Margaret Methodist Church was chartered in 1885 and
the doors opened
souls made professions of faith
holy waters poured on heads and in hearts
sins washed away in the font
babies baptized
young girls married young men
old men blessed before
the Great Beyond
members and converts
walked down to the altar
social holiness marched out of
the building doors into hurting
hearts, hungry bellies, folks in need
it's the Margaret way

Dedicated to my mother, Edwina Ross Halencak Fairchild, my grandmother, Blanche Lisenby Ross, and my mother's Ross family of Margaret, Texas pioneers

Under the Moonlight

I need reality
        to find a place,
        love,
        meaning.

Hallowed
moonlight feeds me
slakes my thirst
feels my flesh
            until orgasm releases.

I submit to dreams.

The circle begins anew.
        First to finish
        Over and over
            until Sabbath's darkened light
                sinks into heavenly hues.

I need reality
        to find a place, love
            with you, I have everything
                I'll wake into a dream under the moonlight.

The Killer

The pusher saw his fate, and it was not good.
It was time for the needles.
Strapped on a table in front of the victim's
family, they waited.

Three years ago,
the killer smelled
blood after he held the
knife.
The kid was pierced into the
heart. Life force flowed onto
the sidewalk near the meth
house.
The victim's friends screamed; users watched.

At the end of his day,
with the needles in his
veins, justice was served.

Banquet 1934

I am starved.
Chicken-fry me a jackrabbit, please.
It's hungry days, you know.
Stomachs want rabbit gravy and mashed wild roots.
Pass me some pig lard for Grandma's crusty
bread, made gleaned grains from neighbor's
ground.
I'll pick mustard greens from the bar ditch.
I'm thirsty and I need sweet tea with a sprig of
mint if we had any tea leaves.
My belly begs for cobbler with clabber, if we had any fruit.
Need a sack of sugar-- too bad I cannot afford it.
Yes, this will be a meal fit for field hands,
if we had any groceries.

Chop Weeds, Clean the Pool on Main Street

I begin my weekend
grubbing weeds,
mowing already manicured grass.
Driving my pick-up truck to Wichita Falls for
chemicals to maintain my pristine pool.
Parties and weekends are waiting with anticipation.
Neighbors and guests attend with mental memo pads
to write the good, the bad, and the occasion weed.
They observe to determine my state of mind-
they know that if my yard is perfect,
then I am content with life and Enlightenment.

From a Shoebox in the Attic

I found an old photograph in a forgotten shoebox
tucked away in a flapper's attic.
I noticed the rouge, painting the cheeks of a young girl
captured in the still-life moment;
the 1920s curls framing the smiling face of an angel.
The glow of happiness and fun and adventure, caught on
film by some camera,
long gone and discarded.
That smile- a look I now wish that I could have seen more
often on the wrinkled face
when she was alive.
    Grandmother, solemn, once young.

We Are Sharecroppers

men in fields
sweating from heat
without water
longs for time to have supper and
ready for bed
the day had been heavy
struggling for the fall
harvest
summer sun sucking up all
moisture
with heads bowed and eyes closed
the family was praying for surviving
crops
dad and his dad before tending plowed clay
armpits smell like hard work without a stock tank for swimming or bathing
damn greedy
Carpetbaggers owning
our land
Sharecroppers-that's who we are

Septic Tears

> *The rain has*
> *filled the*
> *birdbath Again,*
> *almost*
> --Jack Kerouac

Adamic defects
mourn rain into
harden hearts.
Death and destruction loom
with poisoned waters for the
birds. Silence covers the earth
while tears look for a way out.
Existence tries to find its
way but does not.
Mouths digest venom from the Garden.
Where are the showers of blessings?
When does the rainbow peek?
from the dark pall?
When the septic veil is removed
and we'll see the new Earth.
Only then, we'll see the birds' smiles.

> The supreme reality of our time is
> the vulnerability of our planet
> -John F. Kennedy.

Flatlands Poet

I am a poet of the flatlands.
From the dusty plains, I write an
homage to flight towards the unending
sky.
My words whirl around my mind like a chick
caught up in spring storms.

I am a poet of the flatlands.
I chronicle days, dreams, and beasts of
toughened wastelands.

I write poems touching hearts
and ushering in change.
I pen verses making grown men cry
and bastions crumble.

                    I am the mockingbird soaring,
                    resting among the needles of
                    cactus,
                    ascending to the flowering crepe myrtle:
                    soft, sweet, supple, like a mother's
                    breast.

      In the snow of winter, I lament prayers
      from a pained heart.
      Within the storms of sleet,
      Heaven appears elusive.

Then comes the Spring and I revel
within the marvels of the mating calls,
the building of nests,
An abundance of seeds.

I am a poet of the flatlands.
Within my being,
I fly to the ends of the universe.

I am a flatland poet.
My passion has no
limits.

Poem for Music Man

He touched his Paramour with fingers inside her
body; their souls
made love with
        Music.

Piano Man sensed her explosion and responded
      with melodies and Music

Night heat pierced with passion,
delivered out of dark skies with
        Music.

They swam rippled streams;
smelled fragrances of joy;
tasted garden's sweet songs with
        Music.

What Would Ginsberg Do

HOWL!

those who have ears
let them hear and beat it out
a crazy world gone mad

change it

HOWL from your

lungs
and powerful ceilings will
crack like Wicked Witch of the West's mirrors

run down the streets
conquer the citadel of the
damned

risk your HOWL like Allen's
smirk

Pennies in a Jar

Days. Weeks. Years. Dotage.
Demise is not tragic, but
thrilling. I'm on a great
journey.
Living a dream with smiles
  and sorrows,
   laughs
and
tears.
I survive with
memories, without
regret.
Can't wait for the next
penny in the jar.

Campsite Stories

I enjoy campsite BBQs, birthday parties, guys-night-
outs, and so forth near the banks of the Pease River.
Friends and I drive up through the
pasture to the Ross Springs and carry
provisions especially the beer- "damn
straight," as we say. Some will cook
"greasy taters"
while others will grill wild hog backstraps and chicken.
Stargazers watch the crowned tip of the moon,
others just listen to winds, and reflect on days
gone by. We all talk smack, cuss, spit, piss in the
river bed, sit around the campfire, and do
nothing.
Farm boys and old men--"wanna be age 21"-- talk
with rivers of conversation:
sex, wheat prices, school board election, taxes,
religion, and national politics.
That's how we roll.
After cases of beer, there is a deluge--let the sparks begin.
The designated Security named Tiny pockets all the
keys for the remainder of the evening.
Don't mess with Tiny.
No sweat, our wives and Sheriff love big, bad-ass Tiny.

It is the guy's night
      out, and
                            I dig it.

Damn the Darkness

In the heart of the night,
quaking under the covers,
alone,
without wisps of gentle
breezes, it's only warming air.

Haloes circle my soul to wrap me from the darkness.

    I am fearful.
        rescue me
            from the night sky
                until morning comes.

Looking for the Light

Sitting on the ledge on the bluff
looking toward the East, waiting for the sun.

It will fill our souls with Light
And fill our emptiness.

Rays penetrate the darkness.
The abyss opens, and blind
eyes see.

I know that we are part of the Universe
escaping from the imploding star.

Faces

I awaken in the witching hour of the
night. The room is dark.
Lonely lights creep through the curtain. I see
silhouettes encroaching into the bedchambers as
the room embraces its persona.
I crawl out of bed and head for a
beer to appease my internal
demons.
As I walk toward the
kitchen, past the bedroom
furniture,
I notice the shadow of a
man.
                    It is I.
Staring into the cracked mirror I notice that I am not
alone. I recognize them.
I am looking at the ghosts of my past.
We recognize ourselves in the reflections peering back.
I see the myriad of souls defining at that moment. Faces
of wonder.
Hope.
I turn around and smile at the ghosts of my
past.
I am looking into the faces of my future.

Hoover Texas

Vacant home boarded.

Alley behind the abandoned hotel,
where mottled black bitch
is surrounded by
her starving
pups.
Town drunk collapsed,

as he watched the death march on
Main Street.
Breezeless air smells like rotting fields.

No children have been delivered for 40 years.
Local octogenarians segregated into
the nursing home located thirty miles away.

Dust Bowl sands entombed the streets like a vagrant casket.
Cries from the cemetery welcome the last residents.
Welcome to Hoover
Texas. Come back,
ya hear?

This Place

The single bulb dimly glows
from the ceiling.
I stare at it for hours on end,
waiting to burst light from
its dull source.
I continue to wait.
It does not come.

This Place. Lying on
my back, staring
upward.
My body is clutching the
floor. My spine- -holding on f
or life. I am here alone with
no sounds other than my
beating heart, and my
shallow breath.

From this position and in this
location, I can smell the moldy
surroundings.
I can taste the street dirt from shoes
shuffled on the dirty carpet.
The pallet is my creation.

This setting does not
inspire me to go on much
longer.
The attic is where I have shut
myself off from the world.

This place,
in my mind,
where I am no longer alive,
but certainly not dead.

This place.

Contemplation in Summer

Do not disturb me
I tread holy
ground
Pease River called me back
home.

Sacred soil, christened
by tears of joy
I'm alone with my dried River
Immersed in peace, and bliss.

Toiling no longer
Time stands still within my soul
Meditation, rest.

Man, I've Got the Beat

I missed the Beat Generation.
The 21st Century is too tight-assed, racist, and hawkish.

I need some rhythm and blues, jazz, and poetry.
I demand beat and bop and freedom and snapped
fingers, Kerouac, Ginsberg.
I'm looking for bliss, sex in the alley, swimming nude.
Surfing the waves of spontaneous poetry.
Hearing voices through bongos and herbs.
     Because
          Man, I got the Beat.

Visions on Medicine Mounds

Four Mounds on the Rolling Plains; and they
whispered: "There is no past only present." I
named the Mounds "Merely Now"
and I sang a sacred song to the lands

my song is off-key
echoes, whispers, shallow breaths
Medicine Mounds heard

Picnics under the cottonwood trees' shadows,
masked from the sun
Children laughed as they
dipped into the cooling river
water Mounds invited folly
and mirth, love, and romance.

Mounds, sacred, river
We obeyed the earth's spirit
Evening sky prayed

On Pease River banks,
I collected healing cedar berries.
At the foot of the largest
Mounds,
I picked desert sage for burning and cleansing.
Salt Cedar's pink perfume floats in the dry,
hot air along the Pease.
I'm a part of sacred lands.

Pleasures

Simplify.

Little things bring life to full bloom.
Ablaze the field's colors, misty breath.
Sipping coffee on the back porch.
Awake!
    Arise! It's Springtime!

Pleasures.

Special touches. Crazy laughs.
Naps on Sunday afternoons.
Playing like infants.
Holding small objects. Marbles.
Engage!
    Be in the moment!

Fortuity.

Stroll on lost trails.
Dinner with new
friends.
Seining for minnows.
Explore hidden
dreams.
    Abandon!

Find your inner child!

Fiery Hell

The bloody moon covers our
sun and waits for fiery hell
when the blood moon covers our sun.

Unlocked Satan explodes
the world with devilish fun
without loving thoughts.
There are no prayers to tell.
The bloody moon covers
our sun and waits for the
fiery hell.

My Mesquite Tree

At a young age, I was a tree monkey-like Tarzan and
envisioned swinging limb from limb with Cheetah the
Ape and Jim Tom, my Margaret, Texas friends.
It was a mighty tree in Margaret and my watermelon
stand under my Eiffel Tower Tree.
Mesquite Tree trunks were gnarled but stable,
strong enough for my treehouse.
After leaving the yellow school bus at about
3:30, I'd climb on that tree,
looking for watermelon buyers.
$1.50 each, or so I remember.
Charleston Grays or Black Diamonds.
Even cantaloupes.
I remember the feathery leaves and thorns on
my mesquite tree. Mother made me wear
shoes to protect my feet from thorns.
Jim Tom Smith and I would scurry into the
treehouse. Margaret was Africa, we imagine.
We'd chase tigers in an old lady's yard.
Natives tried to tie us to the stake
Then we'd beat them up.
We'd throw knives at the tree
target. The tree did not mind.
Other than Cheetah, Jim Tom,
and the Mesquite, they were my
best friends. They were fond
memories of my childhood and
I'll cherish them in my heart.

Thunder Clouds

Fields laugh for joy when
the earth opens for rain.
Thunder breaks for the new day
within gray
canopies.
Flowers smiling.
Pecan trees spout tassels.
Embryos from the seeded
plants touch the heavens.
Dayspring of the new season
dances in the puddles in green
fields.
Fertile soils did their job,
raising hands in praise for the bounty.

Dark Night Sky

The night air is cold on a winter
respite, and the northeast wind is
screaming, blowing,
bringing you here.
I am miserable without you.
When we are apart, I am sick in
body and mind, and soul.
Together, we are warm and filled;
it's a tropical island
where we are together
under the Dark Night sky.

Margaret's Sandy Loam

When I pass, I will have no regrets
The blaze will only consume the
chaff
and I will devise and bequeath my bounty
of the Harvest to the Universe

Ashes to ashes
When I go to glory land
Will God smile for me?

Where Planted

At the edge of Pease River,
Mother Nature planted cottonwood trees.
A wandering family found a special homestead and
embraced the mottled cottonwoods living in sandy loam.
Young saplings grew into clouds,
providing shelter for traveling cardinals,
held the shifting sands in the predestined place,
caressed twirling winds,
sang wisps of airbrush across green
leaves, tasted waters seeping into thirsty
ground.
Generations marveled at the trees' determination to
survive, as they smiled and watch the solace of the trees'
strength. The cottonwoods' mantles surrounded the
pioneer family for over one hundred years and I was one
of the cottonwood trees planted near Pease River
for their future.

Not Give In

Dragging myself to
the mountain top still
feel numb
can't walk any longer

    but I do and I will

Crawling to the mountain top
entrance to the wounds of my
back but I go on-
    on to the mountain top

I will never give in to the
valley where I was
Must go higher and higher
to live in freedom
    push through the pain

I view the mountain top
See it from afar
Inch by inch
scratch the rocks
to reach the top

    Not give in

Picture

I'm the canvas of His landscape, the beauty of God.
    Clouds are my thoughts.
    Sunrises radiate from His
    eyes.

I reflect on Creation with green
pastures, the face of sunflowers,
wheat berries in His field.

    Is this the legacy of my life?

        The picture, the poise,
           the strength of my
        existence I wait for the smile.

Addiction Is My Name

Dedicated to a close friend…

My name is Addiction and I'm a
fisherman, sailing on troubled waters,
dragging my lines on the bottom of the sea
and fishing with a barrel of chum for a net
full of fellows.

I smile and laugh when I pull them onboard
my boats.
Peering for hollow souls is my passion
and I love it.

Are you slaking with a powerful thirst?
Hobbling on sinking sand?
I'll take care of
you.
I promise.

Ahoy mates:
we will drown our sorrows.
Together, we will board the
Titanic.

Harvest

Growing older has its possibilities.
Spring is the planting season
      as the world waits for the harvest-
      baskets full of ripe fruit,
    wine bottles uncorked,
          sipping the drink on the vine
          with slices of cheese and pears
            on December wakes and Rosaries.
After golden grain's funeral-
                they are bread for heaven

I Thirst

I'm Thirsty

I'm tired.
I'm thirsty.
Give me a drink
of water before I die.
My mouth is parched-
dry as a bone on desert sands.
Let me sit beneath a shade tree
and rest from my yoke.
Heavy and broken underneath
your repression,
 I'm hurt,
I'm tired,
I thirst for freedom.

Opened

Open the shutters allowing the sun's radiance.
New day's portal opens, and the new world
starts again, pour a cup of coffee, then smile-
                chasing night's shadows away.
Time for reflective
moments-
      mornings alone,
      silence with my thoughts,
      pen in hand, scripting
            adventures,
            blessings,
            prayers,
            fresh experiences.

Black Hole

Loss.

It's like a dead star swallowing existence-
        no place to hide
                no way to run
                          from the vacuum.
Candles snuff the whisper.

Torches must carry the light from the
pit and the star will be reborn.

Poet's introduction to his haiku

Haiku is a traditional style of Japanese poetry in which seventeen syllables are written in three lines. Western, American, and "Beat Generation" haiku are different. As defined by Jack Kerouac,

"Above all, a haiku must be very simple and free of all poetic trickery and make a little picture and yet be as airy and graceful"

The poet's haiku is not always "traditional," but his style is sometimes sensual, personal, and intentionally outside the norms.

♦

Early coffee time
       I dragged myself out of bed
PLEASE leave me alone

♦

Shut the fricking door
       WHAT THA...., you finished my last beer!
I'm Thirsty!

♦

(The following haiku is for field-hand Red Necks and they will understand.)

I will name the bar:
       Honey, I am "AT THE FARM'
I will be home soon

♦

Riding on a cloud
       Looking beyond blue heaven
Found my lucking star

♦

Saturday night sky
       Grilled steaks, sizzle, mesquite steam
Smells of my hometown

♦

Kisses of life, taste
       Our dirt roads blow sandy loam
Park at night 'neath moon

♦

Oh no, why?
       On the first date, she just ... OOPS!
I unzipped my fly

♦

Naked and frisky
      Is it time to call my wife?
Sweetheart, come-here-NOW!

♦

Sweet dreams in our hearts
      I'll sleep with you very soon
My love, till will come

♦

Not too cold to swim
      the pool is ready to rock
let us get naked

♦

Pregnant pollen clouds
      Desert skies fill hungry plants-
Orgasmic prayers

♦

Bohemian spring
      The air breathes fresh like the fields
My heart waits for her

♦

Typed into my smile
      The answer was quiet and mellow
Never harsh, never

♦

A cup of coffee
      Poet mind, alone again
Pen in hand

◆

Alone, sipping tea
      The shutters are now open
Sun begins shining

◆

Cacti and mesquite
      Rising across the parched lands
Looking for rivers of life

◆

Stars and Bars, statues
      Old days repeat the South
Again, bitter herbs

◆

The thorns pricked my flesh
      Red roses, mesquite, cacti
Bleeding, pain, remorse

◆

Clouds cloister the shade
      Salvia slakes on damp banks
Nesting beds of soil

◆

Delicate flowers
      Sequestered pool, spent foliage-
Birds mouth prayers, awe

◆

A cup of green tea
      Poetical thoughts again
Pen in hand

♦

Fountain softens skin
      High mountain breath fills dry
lungs Coolness, my cocoon

♦

Afternoons with sun
      Walking in the neighborhood
Smiles & songs with good friends

♦

Black Wall Street matters
      Why White Power remains?
Restitution now

♦

It's time to write
      When I find my special
pen, my soul gets giddy

The Center of Town

The social life of this small town
happens in a place among cotton swabs and
prescriptions. Between rows of men's underwear and
greeting cards, cough syrup, and Tylenol.
Grumpy old men and hired hands,
gather around tables and chairs
with seats well-worn by those dropping by for a cup of coffee and
discussions.
Men debating issues of the local high school
or who deserves to sit in the Oval Office,
can be heard from corner to corner of the
Pharmacy.
Friendship takes on a special meaning,
for the regulars, from early morning until five o'clock, when the
sidewalks are rolled up and stored for another day at Shaw's
Pharmacy.

Roll On, Mighty Pease

The scouts sent forth to find Paradise for
wide-eyed families moving west.
Pilgrims asked the scouts to find the land of milk and
honey, the Valley of Euphrates.
Pioneers wanted a place of freedom and
And the scouts found it.
They saw Niagara Falls in the middle of
the Rolling Plains of Foard County,
located next to the Wichita River,
as hardy as the Amazon
River, as beautiful as the
Nile.
It was a site where they could build
schools like Alexandria,
homes like marble palaces,
and churches like St Peter's
Square. They loved the falls,
cascading over hard stones.
Farmers and ranchers could herd
cattle, sow wheat,
tend the pecan groves,
built churches like Rome.
Life was good for hundreds of years
and they thanked God for the
miracle.

The Tuba Beat

*Dedicated to Kelsey Lien,
"Mr.
Manccordian"*

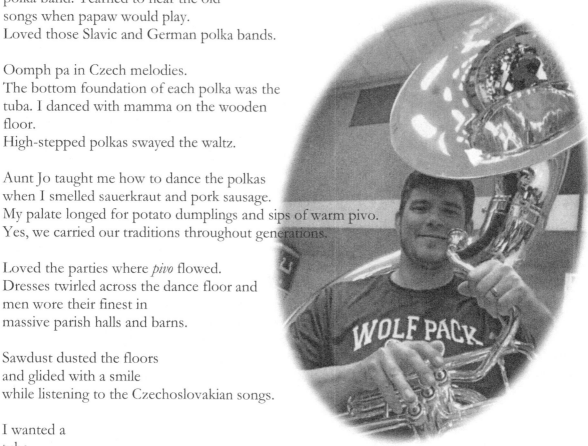

I begged for a tuba
because I wanted to join a Czech
polka band. Yearned to hear the old
songs when papaw would play.
Loved those Slavic and German polka bands.

Oomph pa in Czech melodies.
The bottom foundation of each polka was the
tuba. I danced with mamma on the wooden
floor.
High-stepped polkas swayed the waltz.

Aunt Jo taught me how to dance the polkas
when I smelled sauerkraut and pork sausage.
My palate longed for potato dumplings and sips of warm pivo.
Yes, we carried our traditions throughout generations.

Loved the parties where *pivo* flowed.
Dresses twirled across the dance floor and
men wore their finest in
massive parish halls and barns.

Sawdust dusted the floors
and glided with a smile
while listening to the Czechoslovakian songs.

I wanted a
tuba.
Still do.

Dying Gaul

(a poem inspired by The Dying Gaul or The Dying Gladiator,
a marble statue, commissioned by Attalus I of Pergamon
between 230 BC and 220 BC.)

The proud Gallic combatant was
swimming in a pool of blood.
      His blood.
The crushing army gazed at the
soldier lying on the soil of
death,
naked in front of his enemies.

This fierce beast of a
man was dying from his wounds.

He attempted to pick up his weapon
with his strong hands, but he was defeated.

Muscular legs tried to raise the body
to finish the deliverance from the horde.

He could not.

I wondered what he was thinking
before his demise.
    Fear of
      eternity?
    A noble
    death?
His beloved homeland?

Eternity would never know.

I killed the Gaul
in the bloody
battle.
I respected him.

Saint Joseph's Catholic Church

When I see the structure, I think of Czech
traditions.
This hallowed stucco sacred place has been the essence of
The family for generations.
I see my dad's spirit seated in his special
pew. I smell the aroma of incense during
funerals.
I imagine uncles' and aunts' Baptisms
pouring onto young heads like descending
of the dove.
I see the Host Becoming Body, Blood,
Soul, and Divinity of Eternal Father's
begotten Son.

Prayers. Meditations. Traditions.
I'm a descendant of a charter member.
St. Joseph's Church-
I carry on for our Faith.
My family.

Grand Finality

grand finality on the cusp of ending,
world view in times of trouble,
do we see the big picture?
promotes inequality?
preach the cult of civil war?
grand finality on the verge of life.
world view on the edge of extinction.
we know   execution   lost humanity and
              stormed democracy.

Fragility

Downpour washed muddy
footprints from his courtyard.
His playful romp in soaked, chilly fields,
and smiled.
Memory was a keepsake as a
token of days gone by.

He remembered muddy steps
when impressions of barefoot
trolls in amongst the wet green
and azure fields.

When the glum dark hound nipped
ankles, * he removed his shoes,
deeply into the cool, damp sod.

Beautiful memories showered back
like the flood upon his beloved
trail.
He would smile for a season
until the hound clutched his throat
and ripped it open.

Memories are like shooting stars:
night sky witnesses a bright point of
light, followed by flickers, then
darkness- damned darkness.
His empty soul chased him
into black holes of imploding stars.

The tenderness of his life
swallowed into the hellish abyss
and life transformed
into mere dried, cracked mud.

The black dog is an effective metaphor because depression can feel like an ominous, long-suffering presence tracking your every move. The black dog of depression represents the gradual overtaking of the things you once loved, the person you once recognized in the mirror, or the life you once lived.

My Czechoslovak Grandparents

I can see my grandfather's eyes beyond the
horizon with a blue tint and a smothering smile.
Mirrors reflected his deep wrinkles and small stature, graying hair.
Pronounced forehead with intellect.
Loving music and laughter.
I can see my grandfather's
determination to take care of his own.
His pose demanded strength, stature, and
unconditional love for his family.
Grandfather loved sauerkraut, dumplings, and his accordion.
I can hear my grandmother's laughter.
Her beautiful face was special.
I can see her courage and poise.
She knew how to make amazing
Czech-style chicken noodle soup,
kolaches, and potato dumplings with sauerkraut. I'm thankful for
my grandparents' endearment of
family, friends, and our culture.
Memories hold inside my heart, in
my soul, in my heritage.

Time Moving On

reality fearing
demons   piercing   into
soul's   inferno   weighing
in   minds   storms   with a
dark gloom
moon never glowing
walking through a series of pressure
gazing at the valley of grief
finding for gates of
existence questioning
authority entering times of
change
clocks turning off
morphing into a better person
looking in the mirror
with head holding high
seeing Dream River

bright star, flowing for itself own glow
bending the universe

White Side of Town

We're
proud.
We're loud.
Holding King James Bibles,

      clutching
        guns   to
                save   Our
                        Beloved
                                Country.

We are not
Black.
Not mud people.
Not Muslim.
Not Jew.
Not
queer.
   Just red, white, and blue Americans.

Brothers:
Hold your head up high,
march on the streets,
fight for our cause--
      our way of life.

Forefathers told stories of their past.
Told they'd raised guns and knives
to kill Yankees
     like sick animals.

Told Rebels how they sliced enemies'
     throats from ear
         to ear
             and laughed.

Told about Yankee battlefields with rotting flesh,
         sweet aroma s to nostrils.

They were glorious times.
        But now,
                it's our turn.

Ants Before the Storm

I was a child with a curious mind,
with wonder and awe.
Lived in a lonely place,
with rugged nature, rocks, plants, and
insects watching horny toads
consuming ants and asking myself,
"Why?"

Observing creation is my
passion. Wanted answers.

My home was in the middle of nowhere.
Few friends so my best buddy was
Imagination. About age ten or so, I traveled by
my bike, bagged with warm Cokes and a
package of sunflower seeds from Russell's
Country Store, located in Downtown Margaret,
Texas on a dusty, unpaved street.

On Sunday afternoon adventures,
I peddled my bicycle on country
trails around the village of
Margaret, located in the northwest
drylands of Texas and populated
with pastures of cactus, and
rattlesnakes on sandy loam and
clay. Carried my backpack full of
my treasures.
It was a precious trove: unusual rocks, arrowheads, and bones.

When I found an earthen mound,
I observed the ant's behavior and took
notes. Before the rain, when West Texas
green clouds billowing toward the field,
I smelled moisture in the air,
ants would bring leaves and
dead grasshoppers into the
bunker, fill underground
storage, and protect the Queen
and her eggs.

Found the
answer.
Survival.

sine die

Are you waiting for the end?
I will let you know.
Maybe.

Book Club Discussion Questions

1. After reading his poetry, what is the significance of the title, "Raw and Personal Without Apology?"

2. Prose poetry allows a poet to experiment with emotions and originality. It provides poetical narratives delivering thoughts, lost love, the human condition, and social injustice. The poet addressed other several issues, such as bullying, physical and emotional disabilities, social skills, relationships, and the world. Please discuss these situations.

3. Did you appreciate his prose poetry endeavors? His nontraditional indentions, sentence structure, punctuation, embedded haiku, and pregnant pauses?

4. Why do you think he used an unusual grammar style?

5. The poet believes "in-your-face" poetry challenges himself and readers to think and explore poetry. How did he accomplish that?

6. Did his poetry offend you in your politics, morality, worldview, or in any other way?

7. Why did your group choose his collection?

8. Does your group like or dislike his prose poetry?

9. Which was your favorite poem?

10. Would you like to speak with him about his work?

Contact Information

940.655.4158

artist@srcaccess.net

Daryl Ross Halencak, Post Office 998, Crowell, Texas 79227

About the Poet

DARYL ROSS HALENCAK is a poet, writer, and activist. His poetry and articles were published in Elegant Rage, Speak Your Mind-poems of protest and resistance, Elegant Rage, A Celebration of Poetry: 90 Poems for 90 Years, Ain't Gonna Be Treated This Way, Dagon Poet Review, NonDoc, Cesky Dialog, Ceske Stopy, and others. He took a short sabbatical in Prague, Czech Republic while working on a Czech-Texas magazine. Mr. Halencak was a reader of his works in San Francisco, Albuquerque, Seminole Oklahoma State College, Woody Guthrie Poets, Oklahoma City University, Wichita Falls Poetry Society, Foard County Poetry Festival, and other venues.

He briefly lectured in an advanced composition class at Oklahoma City University. Daryl attended Iowa Workshop and Red Earth MFA Creative Writing Program.

Daryl Ross Halencak was living a full life as an attorney, an elected official, a man active in community charities, and running the family farm in rural Texas until about-face: diagnoses of cancer, stroke, and MS interrupted his life. His survivor instinct propelled him in a new direction.

A native of Crowell in the Rolling Plains, he is a fifth-generation resident of that special landscape, Foard County, Texas. He is on a spiritual adventure, making the most of every day in his world, a world he loves. Daryl and his wife, Jane, reside in the rugged and untamed lands of cows, cacti, and sandy land in the Free State of Foard County.

Made in the USA
Middletown, DE
19 November 2022